MACMILLAN READERS

**ELEMENTARY LEVEL**

NORMAN WHITNEY

# The Stranger

AF172932

macmillan
education

Macmillan Readers is a series of engaging narrative texts designed to stimulate learners while enhancing their language skills, building literacy and boosting reading confidence. Through captivating stories and fascinating cultural themes, learners will explore a diversity of scenarios that foster vocabulary expansion, comprehension skills and a lifelong love of reading.

**The right reader at every stage**
Tailored to each learner's stage of language proficiency, our six levels feature text adapted to match the skill level. With controlled vocabulary and grammar, learners can read freely and immerse themselves in the story. When more challenging words are introduced, either the text will provide sufficient context to aid understanding or a full explanation will be provided in the Glossary.

**Readers for all, anywhere, anytime**
Macmillan Readers are perfect for shared, guided and independent reading. Whether in traditional print, immersive audio or the convenient eBook, Macmillan Readers are equally effective for in-class activities, paired discussions or solo reading at home or on the move.

**Reading for pleasure, knowledge and well-being**
Regular reading and reading for pleasure:
- increases reading confidence, benefiting all literacy skills, not just reading.
- reinforces and enriches vocabulary, providing a variety of contexts.
- expands general knowledge.
- supports concentration, inner reflection and well-being.

Macmillan Readers will inspire a love for reading in English while nurturing essential language skills. Unlock new worlds, expand horizons and embark on an adventure in English!

*(NOTE: While the content of Macmillan Readers is evaluated for age suitability, we kindly remind parents and teachers that they are ultimately responsible for determining whether a particular book is appropriate for their child or student.)*

# Contents

*The People in This Story* 4

1 A Stranger in Woodend 6
2 The Village Meeting 9
3 The Corner Shop 12
4 A Beautiful Customer 14
5 A Page in *Film News* 18
6 A Quick Kiss 20
7 Another Special Order 23
8 The Football Match 27
9 A Secret Weekend 31
10 A Quarrel 33
11 Arthur Riseman 36
12 Anna Waits for News 40
13 The Special Orders Room 46
14 The Special Customers 49
15 31st October 52

*Points for Understanding* 55
*Exercises* 61

# The People in This Story

Dave Slatin

Anna

Peter

Greta Gordon

Mike Bailey

Arthur Riseman

# 1

# A Stranger in Woodend

On Saturday, 31st October, 1964, a man arrived in the village. It was late in the evening. He was looking for somewhere to stay the night. He knocked at a door and a woman opened it.

'Good evening, madam,' the man said. 'I'm sorry it's so late. But can you help me, please? Is there a hotel in this village? I want to stay here tonight.'

The woman laughed. 'A hotel? Here in Woodend? No, sir, I'm afraid there isn't.'

'What a pity,' said the man. 'I'm a stranger here. And I want to see your village tomorrow.'

The stranger was very polite. He was tall and had dark hair. And he had strange green eyes.

'Perhaps Mrs Harrison can help you,' the woman said. 'She has a room. Perhaps you can stay with her. Wait a minute. I'll get my coat, and I'll take you there.'

The woman took the stranger to Mrs Harrison's house. Mrs Harrison gave him a room for the night. He was very glad. It was the last night of October and it was cold.

The next day was Sunday. The man looked round the village. He was very interested in the history of the village. He met some of the villagers and asked them their names.

But he did not visit the church. That was unusual. The church in Woodend was the most beautiful building in the village. But the stranger was not interested in it. He did not go to church that night with all the villagers. It was the first Sunday evening of November.

When the villagers came out of the church, the man had gone.

They had all liked him. The ladies had thought he was very good-looking.

A few weeks later, he came back. It was the first Sunday in December. The villagers were coming out of church. It was cold and dark.

'Hello,' he said. 'I'm back again. It's nice to see you all once more.' His next words surprised everyone.

'Perhaps you can help me,' he said. 'I'm looking for a house. I want to buy a house here.'

'Here?' someone said. 'But why here? There's no work in Woodend for a young man. All the young people leave the village. They find work in Lidney, the nearest town.'

'I'll get a job somewhere,' the stranger said. 'Perhaps in Lidney.'

Then one of the villagers told him about old Mr Smith's house. Mr Smith had died in the summer. His house was empty. It was for sale. The house was on the corner of Main Street and Church Lane.

'I'll ask about the house tomorrow,' said the young man. 'Perhaps I'll be lucky. Goodbye. I'll see you soon.'

The villagers watched him leave. They all saw his car. It was very big and luxurious. He looked rich.

A few days later, Mr Smith's house was sold. And in the middle of December, the young stranger arrived. He moved into the house and worked very hard. He fixed the roof. He repaired broken windows. He painted and decorated. He changed the whole house.

But there was a big surprise for the villagers. On the morning of Monday, 21st December, they saw a big sign on the front of the house. And on the sign were these words:

| THE CORNER SHOP *Proprietor: Dave Slatin* |
| --- |

*A few weeks later, he came back. The villagers were coming out of church.*

## 2

# *The Village Meeting*

The villagers could not believe it. A shop in Woodend! Everybody talked about it. There was once a shop in Woodend, but it had closed twenty years ago.

Some people wanted the shop, but others did not. The villagers met in the evening in the village hall. Everybody was there. Everybody was interested in the new shop.

'The Corner Shop is a good idea,' someone said. 'We need a village shop. We won't need to go to Lidney.'

Then Mrs Harrison spoke. She liked the stranger, Dave Slatin.

'I agree,' she said. 'A village shop is a good idea. It's too quiet here. Woodend needs a shop.'

'Nonsense,' said Miss Brown. She was the village school-teacher. 'Lidney is not far away. There are lots of shops there.'

Soon everybody was shouting. Then Mr Hart spoke. He was a very big man, with a loud voice.

'Listen, everybody!' he shouted. 'We've never had trouble in this village before. We've always been quiet and happy. Now this shop is causing trouble.'

'Let Mr Slatin speak,' someone said. 'It's his shop. Let him speak.'

'Ladies and gentlemen,' said Dave Slatin. 'I don't want to cause any trouble. I'm still a stranger in your village. But I want to be one of you. I want to be your friend. I like the people of Woodend!'

He smiled and a few people clapped. They liked him.

'The Corner Shop will sell lots of things,' he went on.

*The villagers met in the evening in the village hall. Everybody was there.*

'It will sell food and things for the house. Everything will be cheap, I promise!'

Everybody was listening carefully.

'And I have another idea,' he continued. 'I'll sell village products.'

'What do you mean by "village products"?' asked Miss Brown.

'I'll tell you, Miss Brown,' he said. 'I know that you make beautiful bread and cakes.'

Miss Brown smiled. Yes, she did make bread and cakes. Everyone knew that.

'And you, Mr Hart, I've seen your flowers. You grow beautiful flowers.'

Now Mr Hart smiled. Yes, his flowers were beautiful. Everyone knew about them.

'And Mr Everett makes pots,' someone said.

'And Mrs Davies makes dolls,' said another voice.

'And I do paintings of the village,' said old Miss Lucy Gray.

'Yes,' said Dave. 'You can all do something. You villagers are clever. You make lots of things. We can sell them to the tourists. In the summer, Woodend can make a lot of money!'

'But what about the money?' said Mr Hart. 'How will you pay us?'

'That's a good question,' said Dave. 'And here's the answer. You'll bring your things to me and I'll sell them for you. I'll keep some of the profit. You'll have the rest.'

'What a good idea!' said Miss Brown.

'Yes, I agree!' said Mr Hart.

All the villagers agreed. Everyone in the village was happy with Dave Slatin's plan.

The Corner Shop opened on Monday, 4th January, 1965. Soon the shop was busy and Dave needed an assistant.

The new assistant in The Corner Shop was Anna. She started work in late January.

# 3

# *The Corner Shop*

Dave Slatin kept his promises. Things at the shop were good and cheap.

'How does he do it?' asked Mrs Harrison. 'It's winter, but he's selling lots of fruit and vegetables. And they're cheap. I never go to Lidney now.'

The other villagers agreed. The Corner Shop was a success and Dave seemed happy. He paid Anna good wages. Sometimes her friend, Peter, helped at the shop and Dave gave him money too.

Dave advertised in newspapers and the village products sold well. People from Lidney came to The Corner Shop. There were lots of visitors and Woodend became more interesting. The villagers were surprised, but pleased. They were making a lot of money.

Dave lived alone, in a flat above the shop. He was very popular in the village, but no one ever went to his flat. No one ever saw inside it.

At the bottom of the stairs there were two doors. One led into the stockroom. The other door had a notice on it:

SPECIAL ORDERS ONLY: KEEP OUT

The door was always locked. Anna never went into the Special Orders room.

*The new assistant in The Corner Shop was Anna.*
*Sometimes her friend, Peter, helped at the shop.*

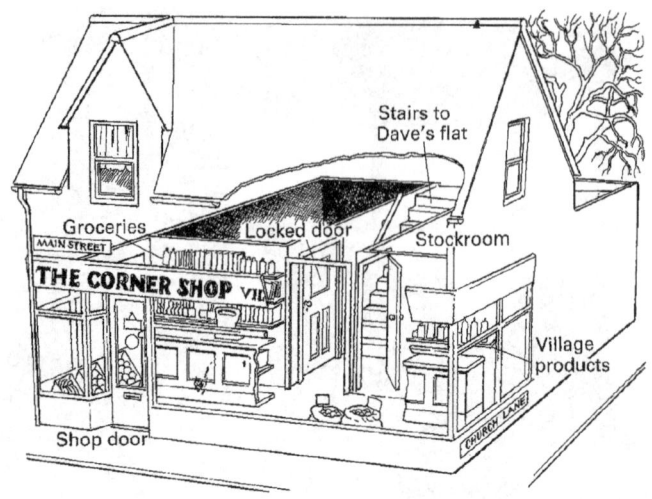

'Why do you lock that room, Dave?' Anna asked one day. 'What's in there?'

'It's for special orders,' he replied. 'Big orders.'

'But you won't get any big orders in Woodend,' said Anna.

Dave said nothing. He did not want to talk about that room.

# 4

## A Beautiful Customer

For three months, everything was normal.

Then, one day in April, an unusual customer came into the shop. The new customer was a very beautiful woman. She was wearing expensive clothes and arrived in a large car.

'Is this The Corner Shop?' the woman asked. She looked round and seemed a little surprised.

'Yes,' replied Anna. 'This is The Corner Shop. It's the only shop in the village.'

'I'm looking for Mr Slatin, the owner of the shop,' said the woman.

'I think he's upstairs,' said Anna. 'I'll go and get him. Does he know your name?'

'Yes, I think so,' was the reply. 'Tell him . . .' The woman stopped.

'Tell him Miss Gordon is here. Miss Greta Gordon.'

Anna was amazed. 'Are you Greta Gordon, the film star?'

'Yes, that's right.'

The woman smiled, but she was nervous.

'Wait a minute,' said Anna. 'I'll tell Mr Slatin that you're here.'

Anna ran to the bottom of the stairs and called 'Dave! Dave! There's someone to see you!'

'Who is it?' asked Dave from upstairs.

'Miss Greta Gordon!' shouted Anna. 'It's Greta Gordon! The film star!'

'I'm coming!' he said, and he came down immediately.

'I'm pleased to meet you, Miss Gordon,' he said.

'Good morning,' said Greta Gordon. She and Dave shook hands. She had beautiful hands and she was wearing beautiful diamond rings! Anna had never seen so many diamonds before.

Miss Gordon looked round. 'Is this where you work, Mr Slatin?' she asked. Once again, she seemed nervous.

'Yes,' said Dave. 'It's a small place, but it's big enough for me. Please follow me, Miss Gordon.'

*Then, one day in April, an unusual customer came into the shop.*

Anna was surprised. Dave and Greta Gordon did not know each other. He did not call her 'Greta', and she did not call him 'Dave'. He seemed to be in a hurry, and she seemed to be frightened.

Anna watched them. Dave and Greta Gordon went to the back of the shop and into the Special Orders room.

Greta Gordon was a Special Order customer! Anna thought that was very strange. She wanted to tell someone about Greta Gordon. Anna loved films. She wanted to tell Peter about the film star. But she had to stay in the shop.

Ten minutes later, Greta Gordon came out of the Special Orders room. Dave went straight upstairs and Greta Gordon came to the front of the shop.

The film star looked terrible! She was pale. She was crying. Her eyes were red with tears.

'What's wrong?' asked Anna. 'Can I help you, Miss Gordon?'

'No, thanks. I'm all right,' said Greta Gordon.

'Do you want to sit down?' said Anna.

She got a chair and the film star sat down.

'Shall I get the doctor?' said Anna.

'No! No!' said Greta. 'Please tell no one about my visit here. Please tell no one.'

Anna was disappointed. She wanted to tell everyone about Greta Gordon. She wanted to tell everyone about her famous customer.

'I want to give you something,' said Greta Gordon. 'Here's a photograph of me. I'll sign it.'

She signed the photograph and gave it to Anna.

'Please keep this,' said Greta. 'And please keep our secret. Please don't tell anyone.'

'All right,' said Anna. 'I promise.'

The film star kissed Anna. She held Anna's hands.

What a beautiful woman, thought Anna. And what beautiful hands!

Then Anna noticed something. The diamond rings were gone.

## 5

# A Page in Film News

Dave never talked about Greta Gordon. He never talked about her visit to The Corner Shop. One day, Anna asked him about the film star.

'How do you know Greta Gordon?' said Anna. 'Is she a friend of yours?'

'I don't want to talk about her,' Dave replied. 'She was a Special Order customer. Don't ask any more questions about her, Anna.'

So Anna did not ask any more questions. She did not ask about Greta Gordon's Special Order and she did not ask about the rings. Anna kept her promise. She never told anyone about the film star.

Soon it was spring. Anna and Dave were busy. Mr Hart brought lots of flowers to The Corner Shop and Anna sold them to the tourists. There were lots of tourists that year.

In May, Peter asked Anna to marry him. She said yes. They became engaged. They planned to get married in the following year. Now they needed money, so they worked hard and they saved. They were very much in love.

On Saturdays, Peter played football or cricket, and Anna often went to the cinema in Lidney. He enjoyed sports and she loved watching films.

One day, Anna was reading *Film News*. This was a magazine about film stars. She turned the pages. There was a picture of Greta Gordon!

**FILM NEWS**

May 1965

# GRETA GORDON WILL STAR IN 'BEAUTIFUL WOMAN'

The star of Beautiful Woman was Joanna Leigh. But Miss Leigh has broken her arm. 'I don't know what happened,' said Miss Leigh. 'I was in my bedroom. I slipped and fell.'

This will be Greta Gordon's first ...

*(over the page)*

## Joanna Leigh breaks her arm

*Greta Gordon will now be the star of Beautiful Woman. 'I'm so lucky,' Greta told us yesterday. 'I've always wanted the part. I can't believe it.'*

Anna was pleased. What a surprise! *Beautiful Woman* was going to be a big film. And now Greta Gordon had the star part.

Anna wanted to tell Peter about Greta, but she kept her promise. She did not tell anyone.

But she did show *Film News* to Dave Slatin.

'Look, Dave,' she said. 'Here's a story about Greta Gordon. Isn't it great! She's got the big part in *Beautiful Woman*.'

Dave looked at the magazine.

'I don't know anything about films,' he said. 'Is Greta Gordon a big star?'

Anna laughed. 'Big star? Yes, she is! She's terrific!'

Dave did not seem interested. 'I hope she's happy with her big part,' was all he said.

<br>

# 6

## *A Quick Kiss*

Summer tourists were arriving in Woodend. The weather was beautiful and the shop was doing well.

But Anna was not very happy. She often thought about Greta Gordon's visit. Why had she come to see Dave? What had happened to the diamond rings on her fingers?

There was another problem. Anna loved Peter and she was going to marry him. But she liked Dave too. Dave was older, but she liked him. All the women liked him.

But Anna was very close to him all day. In the daytime, Anna was with Dave. In the evening, she was with Peter. Anna was living two lives. One life was with Dave, the other life with Peter.

Then one Friday, Dave surprised Anna.

'What are you doing tomorrow?' he asked her. 'Would you like to spend the day with me? We can go anywhere you like. We can go in my car.'

'I'm sorry, Dave,' said Anna. 'But Peter wouldn't like it!'

'Don't be silly,' said Dave. 'We won't go far! I'll close the shop at lunchtime and we can go to Lidney.'

Anna wanted to go with Dave, but she was worried about Peter.

'Don't worry about Peter,' said Dave. 'He's always busy on Saturday.'

Anna thought for a moment. 'All right,' she said. 'You take me to the best cinema and to the best restaurant. Then I'll come with you.'

'Of course!' laughed Dave. 'Anything you want, Anna!'

So the next afternoon Dave and Anna went together to Lidney. They had a good time. Dave bought Anna a new, expensive dress. Then they went to a cinema and, afterwards, to a restaurant.

Peter played cricket that Saturday. He never knew about Anna's day with Dave. He was playing in another village and returned to Woodend very late.

Dave and Anna were also very late. Dave stopped his car near The Corner Shop. The night was warm.

'Thanks, Dave,' said Anna. 'It was a lovely day.'

'I enjoyed it too,' said Dave. He put his arm round her shoulders and kissed her.

It was a quick kiss. But for Anna, it was wonderful.

*Dave put his arm round Anna's shoulders and kissed her.*

# 7

## Another Special Order

The summer passed. The Corner Shop was always busy. Sometimes, Dave opened the shop on Sundays too. Anna earned a lot of money. Everyone thought that she was happy.

But life was difficult for her. She liked Dave. He was her boss, and he was older than her. But Peter was her fiancé, and he was about the same age. Dave was quite rich, but Peter had no money. Dave bought Anna clothes, and he took her out. Peter did not buy her clothes and never took her anywhere. He was more interested in football. Anna did not like football.

Now it was September. Peter played football every Saturday. One Saturday, there was a big football match on television. Mr Hart had the biggest television in the village and he invited some people to his house. He invited Peter and Anna.

On Friday, the day before the match, Anna was working in the shop all day. At five o'clock, she locked the shop door. Two minutes later, the bell rang and Anna went to the door. There was a young man outside. He was carrying a small case.

'Hello,' she said. 'Can I help you?'

'I hope so,' said the young man. 'I want to see Mr Slatin.'

'I'm afraid that the shop is closed now,' said Anna. 'We are open tomorrow morning.'

'But I've got an appointment,' said the young man.

Then Dave spoke behind Anna. She had not seen him.

'Yes, I've been waiting for you,' said Dave. 'You're late.'

*At five o'clock, she locked the shop door. Two minutes later, the bell rang and Anna went to the door.*

'I'm very sorry, Mr Slatin,' said the young man. 'I was . . .'

'Never mind. Never mind,' said Dave rudely.

His rudeness surprised Anna. The young man seemed afraid.

'But can you see me now?' he asked.

'Yes,' said Dave. 'Come in.'

Dave turned to Anna.

'Anna, it's after five o'clock. You can go home now.'

'I won't be long,' said Anna.

Dave was angry. 'Hurry up and go home,' he said.

But Anna wanted to stay. She wanted to know about the young man. The young man followed Dave to the back of the shop and into the Special Orders room.

Another Special Order! Another Special Customer! Anna waited.

But soon it was half past five. Anna put her coat on and left the shop. She closed the door very loudly. Then she went round the corner, and waited.

Soon, there was a noise. The young man was leaving the shop. Anna could not see him, but she could hear him. He was speaking to Dave.

'Are you sure?' said the young man.

'What do you mean?' asked Dave.

'Is this the only way?' said the young man.

'Yes, it is,' said Dave. 'Don't worry. Everything will be all right. Goodbye.'

Anna heard the shop door close. She came round the corner and saw the young man. He was walking quickly to his car. Anna noticed immediately that he was not carrying his case. She followed him.

'Excuse me,' she said. 'You've forgotten something. You have left something behind.'

*The young man's face was white. It was white with fear.*

The young man turned round. Anna stopped. Suddenly she was frightened. The young man's face was white. It was white with fear.

'Please go away,' said the young man. 'Leave me alone. I want to go home. Leave me alone.'

He got into his car and drove off. Anna stood in the street and watched him. She was thinking.

Why had the young man come to The Corner Shop? What was his Special Order? And why had he left his small case with Dave Slatin?

## 8

## *The Football Match*

The next day was the day of the big football match. Mr Hart had invited about ten people. Anna did not watch the game. She was helping Mrs Hart in the kitchen. They were making tea.

It was a good game and everyone was enjoying it.

At half-time, Peter went into the kitchen.

'Why don't you come and watch the match, Anna?' he said. 'It's really good. Come on!'

Anna laughed. 'No, thanks,' she said. 'I'm helping Mrs Hart. Look, here's the tea. Can you take it in to the others?'

'OK,' said Peter. 'It's a terrific match. Mike Bailey scored a great goal.'

Peter took the tea into the sitting room and the second half of the match started.

The second half was very exciting. Mike Bailey scored another goal after twenty minutes. The score was 2–0.

*Anna did not watch the game. She was helping Mrs Hart in the kitchen.*

Then the other side scored two quick goals. It was 2–2. There were only five minutes of the match left.

'Come on!' shouted Peter. 'Come on, Mike! Let's have another goal!'

In the last seconds of the match, Mike Bailey scored the winner. It was his third goal of the match.

But something was wrong! The other team's goalkeeper was injured. Bailey had been very near the goalkeeper and he had kicked the ball very hard. The ball had hit the goalkeeper's neck.

Mrs Hart and Anna came in from the kitchen.

'What's happened?' said Anna. 'What's wrong?'

'It's Brian Thomas, the goalkeeper,' said Peter. 'He's injured.'

It was serious. The goalkeeper had broken his neck.

Later, they all watched the news on TV. They saw pictures of Mike Bailey's third goal. It was a great goal. They saw the ball hit the goalkeeper. It was an accident.

The TV announcer said, 'And now over to our sports studio for an interview with Mike Bailey.'

They all watched the interview. The TV showed a picture of Mike Bailey and the interviewer.

'Mike,' said the interviewer, 'three goals in one match! How do you feel about that?'

But Mike Bailey said nothing. He could not speak. He tried to speak, but he could not. It was terrible.

The interviewer tried another question. 'Let me ask you about the third goal, Mike. It was a great goal. But how do you feel about the injury to Brian Thomas?'

It was a silly question. The injured goalkeeper would never play football again. Mike Bailey said nothing. He looked very ill.

*The TV showed a picture of Mike Bailey and the interviewer.*

When the interview ended, Mr Hart turned off the TV.

No one noticed that Anna had left the room. Mike Bailey had looked frightened. Anna was frightened too. Mike Bailey and Anna had met before. The day before, at The Corner Shop.

## 9

## *A Secret Weekend*

Anna did not know what to do. She was only seventeen, but sometimes she felt much older. She wanted to ask Dave about Mike Bailey and Greta Gordon. She wanted to know about Special Orders. She decided to wait.

One day, Dave and Anna were alone in the shop.

'How's Peter?' asked Dave.

'He's fine, thanks,' said Anna.

Dave smiled. 'Is he still playing football?'

'Of course he is,' said Anna.

Dave laughed. 'You don't see him very much, do you, Anna?'

'I see him three or four times a week,' said Anna.

'What about weekends?' Dave asked.

Anna replied quickly. 'I don't see him much at weekends. He plays football then.'

'When are you getting married?' asked Dave.

'I don't know,' she replied. 'We haven't decided yet. Perhaps next year.'

'That's a long time.' Dave smiled at Anna. Anna felt afraid. She also felt excited. She did not know why.

'Sometimes you're bored, Anna, aren't you?' said Dave. He looked into her eyes.

'Yes,' said Anna. 'That's true.'

'Why don't you come away with me for a weekend,' said Dave. 'We can go to London.'

A weekend in London! Anna had only been to London once, for a day.

Anna was excited, but she was also afraid. 'I don't know,' she said. 'I must think of Peter.'

'Oh, forget him,' said Dave. 'He'll never know. Come with me and we'll go to the best shops. We'll go to the best cinema. Will you come with me?'

Anna said nothing. Suddenly, she had an idea. She looked at Dave.

'Perhaps I'll come with you,' she said.

'Good!' said Dave. 'That's great!'

'But first,' said Anna. 'I want to ask you something.'

'What do you want to know?' he said quietly.

'I want to know about your Special Orders.'

'Very clever,' said Dave. 'You're a village girl, but you're very clever, Anna!'

'Village girls aren't stupid,' said Anna. 'Now tell me about your Special Orders. Then I'll come to London with you.'

Dave was angry. 'One question – you can ask me one question,' he said.

Quickly, Anna asked: 'Why do people come to you? Why . . .'

'One question! Only one!' shouted Dave.

'All right!' said Anna. 'But don't shout. Tell me. Why do people come to see you?'

Dave thought about his answer. He spoke quietly. 'They come for help,' he said. 'They need help. And I give – no, I *sell* help to them. That's all!'

Anna did not understand. 'What sort of help?' she asked.

'One question!' shouted Dave. 'I've answered your question.'

Anna said no more. She and Dave had made an agreement. Anna had asked her question. Dave had answered it. Dave had invited Anna to London for the weekend. And Anna went with him.

## 10

# *A Quarrel*

Anna enjoyed the weekend. They arrived in London late on Friday evening and stayed at a big hotel. On Saturday they went shopping and in the evening they went to a cinema. On Sunday they went to a park.

They came back to Woodend on Sunday evening. It was the last Sunday in September.

On Monday, Anna went to the shop. It was not so busy now. Summer was over. Most of the customers were villagers. It was a cold autumn. On Monday evening, Peter came to see Anna.

'Hello!' said Anna. 'Did you win on Saturday?'

'No,' said Peter. 'We didn't win. And I didn't play.'

Anna was surprised. 'You didn't play? Why not? What was wrong?'

'I didn't feel very well on Saturday morning. I stayed in Woodend. I was in the village all weekend.'

Anna's face was red. Her voice was quiet. 'Are you feeling better now?' she asked.

'No,' said Peter. 'And you know why.'

Anna tried to look surprised. 'Me?' she said.

'Oh, Anna,' said Peter. 'You know what's wrong. It's you and Dave Slatin.'

'What do you mean – me and Dave Slatin?' said Anna quickly.

'You went away with him on Friday evening. Someone saw you in Dave's car.'

Anna tried to explain. 'Oh, it's nothing!' she said. 'Dave and I went . . .'

'Shut up!' said Peter. 'I don't want to know, Anna. Don't talk about it.'

'But Peter!' said Anna.

Peter did not listen. 'I know he's got a lot of money. He can take you to places. He's from a big city. I'm a poor village boy, Anna! But you must choose. You must choose between Dave and me. You can't have both of us.'

'I know that, Peter!' said Anna. 'And I don't want both of you. But listen, Peter. I want to tell you about Dave. There's something very strange about him.'

34

'You must choose between Dave and me. You can't have both
of us.'

'Dave! Dave! Dave!' Peter shouted. 'You talk about him all the time. I don't want to hear his name again.' Peter turned round and walked out of the room. He left Anna's house.

Now Anna was alone. She was very unhappy. She wanted to talk to Peter. She wanted to tell him about Dave. She wanted to tell him about Greta Gordon and about Mike Bailey. But Peter had left her.

## 11

## *Arthur Riseman*

It was October. It was cold and wet. Anna was not very busy at the shop. She was very unhappy. She was a different girl. She seemed older. She did not go out much. She looked ill.

Most of the villagers knew that Anna had quarrelled with Peter. They also knew that she had been to London with Dave. But no one was able to help Anna. She did not talk to anyone. Before, she had been a happy, smiling girl. Now she was sad and lonely.

She went to the shop every day. She was waiting for another Special Customer.

Anna did not wait long. It was the middle of the month. Anna was alone in the shop. It was almost lunchtime. A middle-aged gentleman came in. He was a big man with a very large moustache. He was well dressed and he was carrying a large briefcase.

'Good morning, miss,' he said politely.

'Good morning, sir,' said Anna. 'Can I help you?'

Anna was very polite too. She was interested in this man.

*She looked at the man's case. It had the letters A.R.I.C.S. printed on it.*

'I'm looking for Mr David Slatin,' said the man.

Anna smiled. 'Are you a salesman?' she asked.

She knew that he was not a salesman. He did not look like a salesman. But she wanted to talk to the man.

The man smiled. 'Yes, I am a salesman,' he said.

That was not true. Anna knew that the man was lying. Then she said, 'Perhaps I can help you, sir. I usually speak to the salesmen.'

She looked at the man's case. It had the letters A.R.I.C.S. printed on it.

'Thank you,' said the man very politely, 'but I have a private appointment. I've come from London and I must see Mr Slatin.'

'I'm sorry,' said Anna. 'He's very busy at the moment. But I'll tell him you're here. What's your name, please?'

The man smiled. 'Roberts,' he said. 'Arthur Roberts.'

Anna went to the back of the shop. Dave was coming down the stairs.

'There's a man in the shop,' said Anna. 'He wants to speak to you.'

'Thanks,' said Dave. And he went to the front of the shop.

'Good morning, Mr Riseman,' said Dave. 'I'm pleased to meet you!'

Anna listened. Riseman! The man's name was Riseman, not Roberts! What a liar!

The man did not look at Anna. 'I'm pleased to meet you, Mr Slatin,' the man said.

'Please come with me,' said Dave.

Mr Riseman followed Dave. They went into the Special Orders room.

A minute later, Dave came out. He came to the front of the shop.

'It's lunchtime, Anna,' he said. 'You can go home now.'

'Thanks, Dave,' said Anna. 'I'm going in a few moments.'

Dave went back to the Special Orders room. Anna did not leave the shop. She waited.

Anna wrote down the letters A.R.I.C.S. She understood 'A.R.' – 'Arthur Riseman'. But she did not understand 'I.C.S.'.

At half past one Anna heard noises. Mr Riseman was leaving. Dave was talking.

'Thank you, Mr Riseman,' said Dave.

'And thank you,' said Mr Riseman. 'You have helped me a lot.'

'Good,' said Dave. 'Goodbye, Mr Riseman. My assistant isn't in the shop, but you can open the door. Goodbye.'

Dave went upstairs and Mr Riseman came into the front of the shop. Anna was sitting quietly in a corner.

'Oh!' said Mr Riseman. 'I thought you had gone home.'

'No,' she said. 'I decided to have lunch in the shop today.'

Anna and Mr Riseman looked at each other. They did not like each other. There was silence. Anna spoke first.

'Would you like to buy some bread, Mr Roberts?' she said.

'Riseman, my name is Riseman,' said the man.

Anna smiled. 'I'm so sorry,' she said. 'Would you like to buy some home-made bread, Mr Riseman?'

'It looks delicious,' said Mr Riseman. He was very polite again. 'Yes, I'll take some, please. My wife will love it.'

'Here you are,' said Anna. She put the bread in a bag.

Then she said, 'You can put it in your briefcase.'

'My briefcase?' said Mr Riseman. 'I haven't got a brief-case.'

'I think you've forgotten it,' she said. 'I'll go and get it for you.'

Anna moved towards the back of the shop. Mr Riseman stepped in front of her. He held her wrists. He was very strong.

'Listen to me,' he said. 'I don't want that briefcase. Leave it there.'

'All right,' said Anna. 'Please, let me go. You're hurting me!'

Mr Riseman let go of Anna and turned towards the door. He left the shop hurriedly. He had not taken his bread with him.

Anna watched Mr Riseman leave. Her hands were still hurting five minutes later.

## 12

## *Anna Waits for News*

Anna waited for some news about Mr Riseman. She remembered Greta Gordon. The film star had visited The Corner Shop. Later, there was news about her in a magazine. Mike Bailey had visited The Corner Shop too. Later, there was a lot of news about him on TV. And now Mr Riseman had visited The Corner Shop. Anna was waiting for some news about him.

All three visitors had been Special Customers. They had all seen Dave. They had all been in the Special Orders

*Mr Riseman stepped in front of her. He held her wrists. He was very strong.*

room, and they had all left something with Dave. Greta Gordon had left her diamond rings. Mike Bailey had left his case. Mr Riseman had left his briefcase.

Anna wanted to find out more about the three "Special Customers". She thought about Mr Riseman. His case had the letters A.R.I.C.S. on it. She understood 'A.R.'. But what was 'I.C.S.'? Perhaps Mr Riseman was a businessman and 'I.C.S.' was his company?

Anna looked in the newspapers. But she did not find anything about 'I.C.S.'. She read the magazines. She listened to the radio. She watched TV. But there was nothing about 'I.C.S.'. Anna heard nothing. She saw nothing.

Then she had an idea. She decided to go to London and find Arthur Riseman.

It was a Friday. Early in the morning, she left a note for Dave. She took the note to the shop.

*'Dear Dave,'* it said, *'Sorry I can't come in today. I'm going to Lidney. I'm buying some things for my wedding. Anna.'*

The note did not tell the truth, but Anna did not care.

Anna took a bus to Lidney and then caught a train to London. She got to Paddington Station at midday.

She got off the train and looked for a telephone box. The telephones were near to the entrance to the station but the boxes were all full.

She stood and waited.

Then Anna saw the letters 'I.C.S.'. There they were! They were on a huge advertisement. Anna had found the answer to her problem.

*International Computer Services!* I.C.S. Perhaps that was Mr Riseman's company.

Soon one of the phone boxes was empty. Anna rang the number 222 8959.

*The letters were on a huge advertisement. Anna had found the answer to her problem.*

'I.C.S. Can I help you?' said a woman's voice.

'Yes, please,' said Anna. 'I want to speak to Mr Riseman. Mr Arthur Riseman. I think he works at I.C.S.'

The woman laughed. 'Works here? Yes, he does!' she said. 'He's the Vice Chairman of the company. Wait one moment, please. I'll get his secretary.'

Then there was another woman's voice on the phone.

'Mr Riseman's secretary. Can I help you?'

'Yes, please,' said Anna. 'I'd like to speak to Mr Riseman.'

'Who's calling, please?' said the secretary.

'Mr Riseman doesn't know my name,' Anna replied.

'Is Mr Riseman expecting your call?' the secretary asked.

'No, he isn't,' said Anna.

'I'm afraid he can't speak to you now,' said the secretary. 'He's at a meeting now and he's flying to Switzerland in an hour's time.'

'But I must speak to him for a few minutes,' said Anna.

The secretary became annoyed. 'That's impossible,' she said. 'But I can take a message.'

'No, thanks,' said Anna. 'I'll call again next week. Will Mr Riseman be back then?'

'Yes, he will,' replied the secretary. 'Goodbye.' And she put the phone down.

Anna had found Mr Riseman's company. But she had not spoken to him.

Anna spent the afternoon in London. She went to see a film. Then she had tea in a small café near Paddington Station. Her train left London at half past six. She bought an evening newspaper, and got on the train.

Anna was tired, but she felt happy. After a few minutes, she looked at her newspaper. Anna was waiting for some news. There it was, on the front page:

44

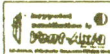

# Evening Standard

# PRIVATE PLANE CRASH NEAR LONDON

*Enfield –
Scene of Horror Crash*

## Six Dead: All from ICS

### ROBERT ARNELL, Enfield

Six people were killed this afternoon in a plane crash at Enfield, near London. The plane was flying to Switzerland.

The passengers were all from International Computer Services (ICS). Among them was Mr Alfred Gluck, the Chairman of ICS.

**'Lucky to be alive'**

Mr Arthur Riseman, Vice Chairman of ICS, told us, 'I'm lucky to be alive. I was at a meeting today. The meeting went on for a long time and I didn't catch the plane.'

Mr Riseman will probably be the new chairman of ICS.

Continued on page 2

## Paint gun vandals raid cathedral

### CANTERBURY TREASURES ARE SPRAYED

**JAMES IRVING**

CANTERBURY, Friday — Canterbury Cathedral was desecrated today with paint spray gun.

It may have been a protest against the Primate's "Fight in Rhodesia" speech for "Peace" was sprayed in blue paint on the Holy Altar.

## Dame Peggy sues for divorce

## Wilson in big row over TV

The Rhodesia independence talks on which the unanimity of the African argument could depend are ending with a great row about how the Rhodesian people should be told that negotiations appear to be failing.

In a confused and rapidly changing situation it seemed it might be the way Mr. Harold Wilson wished.

There was later personal wrangling between Mr. Wilson and Mr. Ian Smith over the terms on which the former may be allowed to appear on Rhodesian television.

## It's here now, the new

# WOLSELEY 1100

test-drive it today—ring Eustace Watkins

## EUSTACE WATKINS FOR WOLSELEY

# 13

## The Special Orders Room

Anna got home about ten o'clock. She turned on the radio and listened to the news. The Chairman of I.C.S. was dead and Mr Riseman was the new Chairman.

Anna did not sleep that night. She was thinking about Dave Slatin and the Special Orders. What were they? What was Dave Slatin doing in that room?

On Saturday morning she went to the shop. Dave said nothing to her. He was angry because Anna had not worked on Friday. He did not ask about her day off, and Anna did not tell him about it.

At eleven o'clock, Dave left the shop. He got in his car and drove off.

Anna was alone. This was her chance! She went to the back of the shop and turned the handle of the locked door.

But the Special Orders room was not locked! Dave had forgotten to lock it. Anna opened the door and went into the room.

It was a small room, dark and hot. Anna turned on the light, but it was not a very strong light.

She looked round the room. There was a small table, two old chairs and a lot of boxes. That was all. Special Orders? There were no order books, no papers, no pencils.

Anna walked round the table. It was difficult because there were a lot of boxes on the floor. Anna opened one of the boxes and looked inside. She found some old magazines and newspapers. Underneath, there were some dirty, old clothes.

But underneath the clothes she discovered some money.

*Anna opened the door and went into the room.*

Lots of money. British money. French money. American. German. There was money from all over the world. Anna was amazed. She had never seen so much money before.

She looked round again and found Mike Bailey's case. It was empty. Then she found Arthur Riseman's briefcase. That was empty too.

Then Anna looked into a bigger box. Inside it were some dolls with broken arms and legs. One of the dolls was very beautiful, but it had a broken arm. Anna put it on the table.

Then Anna found a book about football. Inside there were some pictures of footballers but the pictures were all torn. Anna put the book on the table.

Anna looked into the box again and found some little cars. Most of them were broken. She found a small model aeroplane. It was broken too.

Anna put all these things on the table. What a strange collection! There was the money, the broken doll, the toy cars, the model aeroplane. And there was the football book with the torn pictures. Anna looked at the things on the table.

What were they for? Why did Dave Slatin keep them in this locked room?

Suddenly Anna jumped. There was a noise behind her.

Someone was standing at the door.

# 14

## *The Special Customers*

'What about the diamond rings?' said a voice.

It was Dave Slatin. He was laughing.

'I left the door open for you,' he said. 'I wanted you to go into this room this morning!'

Anna was frightened, but she tried not to show her fear.

'You haven't found the diamonds,' Dave said again.

Anna remembered Greta Gordon's diamond rings. Were they in this room too?

'Here,' said Dave. He came into the room and picked up an old box. He took out the rings and threw them on the table.

'They aren't yours,' said Anna. 'They belong to Greta Gordon.'

'They belong to me,' laughed Dave. 'She gave them to me.'

'But why?' asked Anna. 'Why? Why did Greta Gordon give you those diamonds? And all this money. Who gave you the money?'

'My Special Customers!' said Dave. 'My Special Customers gave me the money. It's mine now.'

'Mike Bailey and Mr Riseman gave you all this money?' asked Anna.

'Yes,' said Dave. 'You have seen some of my Special Customers, not all of them.'

'But why do they come?' Anna asked again.

'These people come to me for help,' replied Dave Slatin. 'I help them and they pay me.'

'But how do you help them?' asked Anna.

Dave Slatin picked up the beautiful doll with the broken arm.

'Do you remember Joanna Leigh?' he asked Anna.

Anna thought for a moment.

'Joanna Leigh?' she said. 'Yes, of course I remember her. She's the actress who broke her arm. Greta Gordon got her part.'

'That's right,' said Dave Slatin. 'This doll is Joanna Leigh.'

Anna felt more afraid. What kind of man was Dave Slatin?

Dave Slatin pointed to a torn photograph in the football book. 'Who's that, Anna?' he asked.

Anna remembered the face. She had seen it on TV.

'Brian Thomas,' she replied. 'He's a goalkeeper.'

'He *was* a goalkeeper,' said Dave Slatin.

Anna was terribly frightened now. Dave Slatin was an evil man.

Dave Slatin moved close to Anna. He picked up the broken aeroplane.

'And what do you think this is?' he asked Anna.

Anna knew the answer, but she was too afraid to speak.

Dave Slatin took Anna's arm and held it tightly. Anna tried to move away. Dave Slatin laughed and held Anna more tightly.

'Listen, Anna,' he said quietly. 'I want you. I need you.

*Dave Slatin took Anna's arm and held it tightly.*

Marry me, Anna. Don't marry Peter. Marry me.'

'No, no,' she cried. 'Let me go. Let me go.'

'But Anna, you still don't understand,' said Dave Slatin. 'I have strange powers. I can give you everything you want.'

He looked into Anna's eyes. 'And my children will have these powers too,' he continued. 'I will give you money and diamonds. And you, Anna, you will give me children.'

Anna was terrified now. She kicked Dave Slatin very hard and he let go of her hand. Anna moved quickly. She ran out of the Special Orders room through the front of the shop and out onto the street. She ran all the way home.

## 15

## *31st October*

When Anna got home, she felt terrible and went to bed. In the evening, Peter came to see her. But Anna was ill in bed.

'I'll come and see Anna tomorrow,' Peter told Anna's mother.

Again, Anna did not sleep all night.

The next day, Sunday, 31st October, was a terrible day for Woodend. Anna stayed in bed. She had a fever and her mother phoned the doctor. The doctor came immediately.

'Anna's very ill,' said the doctor to Anna's mother. 'I'm worried. I don't know what's wrong with her. I'll come back again tonight.'

That afternoon, Peter came to Anna's house. He tried to speak to Anna, but she was too ill. He sat quietly beside her bed.

At about seven o'clock, Peter heard shouting in the street. He went to the window and looked outside. People were running and shouting, 'Fire! Fire! Fire! There's a fire at The Corner Shop!'

Peter ran out of Anna's house and into the street.

There was a big fire on the corner. The shop was in flames. Nobody could see Dave Slatin.

'His car's here!' said Mr Hart. 'Dave must be inside.'

Then the villagers saw him. He was standing at an upstairs window.

'Jump, Dave,' they shouted. 'Jump! Save yourself.'

But Dave did not move. He was standing at the window and he was laughing.

Some of the women in the street started screaming. Mr Hart tried to run into the shop, but the others pulled him back. Flames were leaping up from the shop.

The flames reached Dave Slatin. The villagers saw that he was still laughing. That was the last time they saw him. The flames hid him completely. No one was able to save him and no one ever saw him again.

Peter went back to Anna's house. The doctor was in the kitchen, talking to Anna's mother.

Suddenly there was a scream. They ran upstairs to Anna's room. Anna was dead.

*Then the villagers saw him. He was standing at an upstairs window.*

# Points for Understanding

## 1

1 Why was the stranger looking for a hotel?
2 What was the date?
3 What was the most beautiful building in Woodend? Did the stranger go to see it?
4 What did the village ladies think about the stranger?
5 The stranger came back to Woodend a few weeks later. What was he looking for?
6 What surprised the villagers on the morning of Monday, 21st December?

## 2

1 Why did the villagers have a meeting?
2 Why did Mrs Harrison think that a village shop was a good idea?
3 Why did Mr Hart think the shop was a bad idea?
4 What did Dave Slatin mean by 'village products'? Why were the villagers pleased with the idea of selling 'village products'?
5 'But what about the money?' said Mr Hart. What was Dave Slatin's reply?
6 Why did Dave Slatin need an assistant? Who was the new assistant?

## 3

1 Mrs Harrison said: 'I never go to Lidney now.' Why did she not go to Lidney?
2 Who sometimes helped Anna at The Corner Shop?
3 Lots of visitors came to Woodend. Why were the villagers pleased?
4 Where did Dave Slatin live?
5 One door in The Corner Shop was always locked. What was written on the notice on this door? Did Anna ever go into this room?

## 4

1 Who was Greta Gordon? What did she want?
2 Anna noticed that Greta Gordon had beautiful hands. What did Anna see on Greta Gordon's fingers?
3 Where did Dave Slatin take Greta Gordon?
4 Why did Anna want to speak to Peter?
5 When Greta Gordon came back to the front of the shop, Anna asked her, 'What's wrong?' Why did Anna ask this question?
6 Greta Gordon asked Anna to do something. What did she ask Anna and why was Anna disappointed?
7 Greta Gordon held Anna's hands. What did Anna notice about Greta Gordon's fingers?

## 5

1 Anna asked Dave Slatin about Greta Gordon. What was his reply?
2 Anna kept her promise. Who had Anna made the promise to? What was the promise?
3 Why did Anna and Peter need money?
4 Anna and Peter did not go out together on Saturdays. What did each of them do?
5 Who was Joanna Leigh and what had happened to her?
6 Why was Greta Gordon lucky?

## 6

1 Anna often thought about Greta Gordon's visit to The Corner Shop. What did she ask herself?
2 Anna was living two lives. What does this sentence mean?
3 Anna wanted to go with Dave, but she was worried about Peter.
   (a) Where had Dave asked her to go?
   (b) Why was Anna worried about Peter?
   (c) What was Dave's reply to Anna's worry about Peter?
4 Why did Peter not know about Anna's day with Dave?
5 Dave thanked Anna and kissed her. Was Anna pleased or not?

## 7

1   Anna liked Dave, and Peter was her fiancé. What were the
    differences between the two men in:
    (a)   age?
    (b)   money?
    (c)   taking Anna out?
2   Why had Mr Hart invited some people to his house?
3   One evening the bell rang after Anna locked the shop.
    (a)   Who was outside?
    (b)   What did he have in his hand?
    (c)   What did he want?
4   Why did Anna wait until half past five?
5   Anna left the shop. Where did she go and what did she do?
6   Anna stopped the young man and said: 'You've forgotten
    something.'
    (a)   What had the young man forgotten?
    (b)   Why was Anna frightened when she saw the young man's
          face?
    (c)   What did the young man do?
7   What three questions did Anna ask herself about the young man's
    visit?

## 8

1   Mr Hart and his friends were watching TV. What was Anna doing?
2   What was the name of the player who scored three goals?
3   What happened to Brian Thomas, the goalkeeper?
4   Anna left the room during the TV interview. She was frightened.
    Why was she frightened?

## 9

1 Dave Slatin invited Anna to go away with him for the weekend. Where to?
2 Before Anna agreed to go with Dave Slatin, she wanted to know about something.
  (a) What question did Anna ask Dave Slatin?
  (b) What was his reply?
3 Anna wanted to ask Dave Slatin more questions. What did he say?

## 10

1 Where was Peter on Saturday?
2 Anna wanted to speak to Peter.
  (a) What did she want to tell him?
  (b) Why was she not able to speak to him?

## 11

1 Anna was unhappy, but she went to the shop every day. Why?
2 A man came into the shop carrying a briefcase.
  (a) What letters were printed on the briefcase?
  (b) Who did the man want to see?
3 The man told Anna his name.
  (a) What did the man say his name was?
  (b) How did Anna find out that he was lying?
  (c) What was the man's name?
4 'You can go home now,' Dave Slatin told Anna. What did Anna do?
5 'I'll go and get it for you,' Anna said to the man.
  (a) What was Anna going to get?
  (b) What did the man do?

# 12

1   After Mr Riseman visited the shop, Anna was waiting for something. What was she waiting for?
2   All the three Special Customers left something. What did each one leave?
3   Anna still wanted to find out what the other three letters on Riseman's briefcase stood for.
    (a)  What were these three letters?
    (b)  What did Anna decide to do?
4   Anna found the answer to her problem at Paddington Station.
    (a)  Where did she see the answer?
    (b)  What was the answer?
5   Anna tried to speak to Mr Riseman on the telephone.
    (a)  Where was Mr Riseman?
    (b)  Where was he going in an hour's time?
    (c)  How was he going to travel?
6   Later that afternoon, Anna read about a plane crash in her newspaper.
    (a)  Who had been killed in the plane crash?
    (b)  Why was Mr Riseman lucky?

# 13

1   Who was the new Chairman of I.C.S.?
2   Why did Anna not sleep that night?
3   Why was Anna able to go into the Special Orders room?
4   In one of the boxes, Anna found some old clothes. What did she find under the clothes?
5   In the Special Orders room, Anna found a beautiful doll, a model aeroplane and a football book with pictures in it. What was wrong with these three things?

## 14

1 Why had the door to the Special Orders room been left unlocked?
2 Who had given Dave Slatin the money and the diamonds?
3 'This is Joanna Leigh,' said Dave Slatin, holding the beautiful doll.
    (a) Who was Joanna Leigh?
    (b) What had happened to her?
4 Dave Slatin pointed to the photograph in the football book.
    (a) Who was the footballer in the photograph?
    (b) What had happened to the photograph?
    (c) What had happened to the footballer?
5 Anna knew the answer, but she was too afraid to speak.
    (a) What was Dave Slatin holding in his hand?
    (b) What question did he ask Anna?
    (c) What was the answer to his question?
6 Dave Slatin offered Anna money and diamonds.
    (a) What did he ask Anna to give him?
    (b) What was her reply?

## 15

1 Why was Peter not able to speak to Anna?
2 The flames reached Dave Slatin. What did the villagers see he was doing?
3 What happened to Anna?

# Exercises

## Making Sentences

**Match the two parts of each sentence.**

1 The stranger came to                          was called Greta Gordon.

2 Dave Slatin was young            and they each left something behind.
   and handsome

3 One of the village houses       to marry him.
   was empty

4 Dave Slatin bought the          a small village called Woodend.
   empty house

5 There was a notice on the       because the owner had died.
   locked door:

6 Three people came to the        and changed it into The Corner Shop.
   Special Orders room

7 The famous film actress         and he had an expensive car.

8 Anna began to think that        Anna also died.

9 Dave Slatin wanted Anna         SPECIAL ORDERS ONLY: KEEP OUT

10 When Dave Slatin died,         Dave Slatin was a bad man.

## People in the Story

**Unjumble the letters to find the characters' names.**

| | | |
|---|---|---|
| 1 | NANA | *Anna* ............................... |
| 2 | SIR MEAT HURRAN | ....................................... |
| 3 | BIMLEYAKIE | ....................................... |
| 4 | DON GOER GRAT | ....................................... |
| 5 | TREEP | ....................................... |
| 6 | DEVIL SATAN | ....................................... |

61

# Words From the Story

Unjumble the letters to find words from the story. The meanings are given to help you.

1            **icepals**

Meaning:      not usual or ordinary; particular for one person or thing
               *special*
....................................

2            **cigerroes**

Meaning:      food that you buy from a shop – especially in
packets and tins

....................................

3            **mostrocko**

Meaning:      a room where a shop keeps things ready to sell

....................................

4            **trooperrip**

Meaning:      the owner of a shop or business

....................................

5            **tenpointamp**

Meaning:      a time you have fixed to meet somebody – often
for business

....................................

6            **curtsome**

Meaning:      a person who buys things from a shop

....................................

7            **nonalientrait**

Meaning:      between different countries

....................................

8            **perviat**

Meaning:      for one particular person or group of people only
– not for everybody

....................................

## The Stranger Arrives

Complete the gaps. Use each word in the box once.

> spare   night   unusual   locked   on   and   a   know
> villagers   in   came   of   back   bought   into   ~~where~~
> stay   it   to   hotel

Nobody knew [1] *where* Dave Slatin [2]................. from. His name was
[3]................. . He appeared [4]................. the village [5]................. the
last day [6]................. October 1964 [7]................. he wanted
[8]................. stay for the night.

Woodend was [9]................. small village, and it didn't have a
[10]................. . One of the [11]................. let Dave Slatin
[12]................. for one [13]................. in a [14]................. room.

One month later, Dave Slatin came [15]................. to Woodend and
[16]................. an empty house. He turned the house [17]................. a
shop. He called [18]................. The Corner Shop.

Anna worked for Dave Slatin. She liked him, but she wanted to
[19]................. what was inside the [20]................. room.

## True or False?

Read the sentences. Then write T (True), F (False) or ? (Don't Know) next
to the statements below.

1   The stranger appeared on the last day of October in the evening.

a   [T]   He appeared on 31st October.
b   [F]   The weather was fine.
c   [?]   The room was small.
d   [T]   No one had seen him before.

63

2  Mr Smith had died in the summer. His house was empty and for sale.

a  ☐  It was possible to buy the house.

b  ☐  Mr Smith had died a long time ago.

c  ☐  Nobody was living in the house.

d  ☐  The price of the house was cheap.


3  A new sign on the old house read: THE CORNER SHOP
   Proprietor: Dave Slatin

a  ☐  The shop was at a place where two roads meet.

b  ☐  Dave Slatin was the owner of the shop.

c  ☐  The shop sold both new and old things.

d  ☐  The sign on the house was old.


4  The door to the Special Orders room was locked and only Dave had the key.

a  ☐  Anyone could look inside the room.

b  ☐  The room had only one small window.

c  ☐  Only Dave Slatin could go into the room.

d  ☐  We do not know what was in the room.


5  A young man followed Dave to the back of the shop and into the Special Orders room.

a  ☐  The Special Orders room was at the back of the shop.

b  ☐  Dave went into the Special Orders room.

c  ☐  The young man went into the Special Orders room before Dave.

d  ☐  Dave shut the door of the Special Orders room.

# The Special Orders Customers

Complete the gaps. Use each word in the box once.

> room    businessman    that    came    took    visitor    a
> name    soon    Special    film    broke    neck    footballer
> him    important    save    star    Corner    customers    said
> later    was    day    goals

Three special [1]......................... visited The [2]......................... Shop.

Each customer [3]......................... for a [4]......................... Order.

Dave Slatin [5]......................... them into the locked [6]......................... .

The first [7]......................... was Greta Gordon. She was [8].....................

film star. Her [9]......................... appeared in the newspapers

[10]..................... afterwards. She became the [11]......................... of

a big [12]....................... called *Beautiful Woman* when the original star

[13]......................... her arm.

The second visitor was a [14]......................... called Mike Bailey. The

next [15]......................... Anna saw [16]......................... on TV. Mike

Bailey scored three [17]......................... in an [18].........................

soccer match. The goalkeeper broke his [19]......................... trying to

[20]......................... the third goal.

The third visitor was a [21]......................... from International

Computer Services. He told Anna [22]......................... his name was

Arthur Roberts, but Dave Slatin [23]......................... 'Good morning,

Mr Riseman.' A month [24]......................... the Chairman of

International Computer Services [25]......................... killed in a plane

crash. Arthur Riseman became the Chairman of the company.

# Choose the Verb

Complete the gaps with the correct verb form from the brackets.

Anna got back from London in the evening but she [1](**did not sleep /
has not slept**) ..........*did not sleep*.......... that night. She [2](**thinks / was
thinking**) ................................ about Dave Slatin and the Special
Orders. What [3](**was / were**) ................................ they? What
[4](**was /were**) ................................ Dave Slatin [5](**do / doing**)
................................ in that room?

She [6](**has gone / went**) ................................ to work, as usual, the
next morning. At eleven o'clock Dave [7](**has left / left**)
........................... the shop. He [8](**has got / got**) ...............................
in his car and [9] (**drove / driven**) ................................ off.

That morning, the Special Orders room [10](**did not be locked / was not
locked**) ................................ Anna [11](**opened / was opening**)
............................ the door and [12](**looked / looking**)
............................ inside.

She [13](**began / begun**) ............................ [14](**search / to search**)
............................ through boxes. She [15](**found / was finding**)
............................ money, lots of money. There [16](**is / was**)
............................ also a doll and a model aeroplane. They
[17](**broke / were broken**) ........................... .

Suddenly Dave Slatin [18](**came / was coming**) ............................
into the room. 'Now you [19](**know / have known**) ...............................
he [20](**said / was saying**) ............................ .
'I [21](**have / am having**) ............................ strange powers.
I [22](**use /was used**) ............................ these powers [23](**to help / to helping**)
............................ my special customers. And I [24](**can use / can be
using**) ............................ them [25](**to help / to be helping**)
............................ you too.

66

## Special Occasions

*The Stranger* begins on 31st October. This is a special day in some countries. The occasion is called Halloween. In the past, people believed that ghosts and devils and evil spirits appeared on the night of 31st October.

Halloween is a special occasion for children in Britain and the United States. Do you have Halloween or a Day of the Dead in your country?

In many countries, New Year is a special occasion; but dates and years are counted in different ways in different countries. In America and Europe, New Year is on 1st January. Five hundred years ago, it was on 25th March. In other parts of the world, the first day of the year changes according to the moon. Chinese New Year is in either January or February.

What are the special days in your country? Make a list.

| Special Days in Your Country | Holiday*? (Y/N) | Special Days in Other Countries |
|---|---|---|
| | | *Bonfire Night – Britain* |
| | | |
| | | |
| | | |
| | | |
| | | |
| | | |
| | | |
| | | |
| | | |
| | | |
| | | |
| | | |

* Days when schools and offices close

## Dates and Times

Complete the gaps with *in*, *at* or *on*.

1  Dave first appeared in Woodend .....*on*..... Saturday 31st October, 1964.
2  Anna got back from London late ............ the evening.
3  Dave arrived in the village ............ night.
4  He came back the first Sunday ............ December.
5  He moved into the house ............ the middle of December.
6  ............ the morning of Monday 21st December the villagers noticed a big sign outside the house.
7  The shop opened ............ nine o'clock ............ the morning.

## More Dates

When we fill in forms or take notes, we often use numbers to write a shortened form for dates. For example:

10th January 2024 = 10/01/24

Rewrite the dates below (2–5) in shortened number form. Then rewrite the shortened forms (7–10) as full dates.

| Dates | Shortened number form |
|---|---|
| 1 31st December 2001 | 31/12/01 |
| 2 7th November 2023 | |
| 3 12th September 2010 | |
| 4 5th August 2019 | |
| 5 1st July 1997 | |
| 6 6th July 2020 | 06/07/20 |
| 7 | 09/10/17 |
| 8 | 12/11/22 |
| 9 | 04/05/89 |
| 10 | 02/01/15 |
| Note: In American English, dates are written the other way round: January 10th 2024 = 01/10/24 | |

Macmillan Education Limited
4 Crinan Street
London N1 9XW

Companies and representatives throughout the world

Macmillan Readers Elementary Stranger, The
ISBN: 978-1-035-16642-8
Macmillan Readers Elementary Stranger, The with eBook and Resources
ISBN: 978-1-035-16646-6

First published 1977
This edition published 2025

Illustrated by Annabel Large
Cover photograph by Photographer's Choice

Printed and bound by CPI Group (UK) Ltd, Croydon CR0 4YY
POD 2025